MCR

W9-BJM-575

3 1192 01415 8792

∴ **MATH ALIVE** ∴

TRAVEL
MATH

Pia Awal Dutta

mc **Marshall Cavendish**
Benchmark
New York

Marshall Cavendish Benchmark
99 White Plains Road
Tarrytown, NY 10591
www.marshallcavendish.us

Library of Congress Cataloging-in-Publication Data
Awal, Pia.
Travel math / by Pia Awal Dutta.
p. cm. -- (Math alive)
Includes bibliographical references and index.
ISBN 978-0-7614-3217-3
1. Word problems (Mathematics)--Juvenile literature. 2. Travel--Mathematics--
Problems, exercises, etc.--Juvenile literature. I. Title.
QA63.A93 2009
510--dc22
2008014558

The photographs in this book are used by permission and through
the courtesy of:

LyaC/ Istockphoto: 4-5, Stephen Finn/ Shutterstock: 6, Vidler Vidler/ Photolibrary: 8,
Angelina Dimitrova/ Shutterstock: 9bl, Andr   Klaassen/ Shutterstock: 10-11, Alan
Ward/ Shutterstock: 12, David R. Frazier Photolibrary, Inc./ Alamy: 15, Goydenko
Tatiana/   Shutterstock: 16, Marc V   rin/ Photononstop/ Photolibrary: 18, Daniel
Gustavsson/ Shutterstock: 20, Jarno Gonzalez Zarraonandia/ Shutterstock: 23,
Bernard Breton/ Dreamstime: 24-25, Adambooth/ Dreamstime: 26,
Associated Press: 28,
Illustrations: Q2AMedia Art Bank
Cover Photo: Front: Tischenko Irina/ Shutterstock.
Back: UltraOrto, S.A./Shutterstock.
Half Title: Andre Klaassen/ Shutterstock.
Creative Director: Simmi Sikka
Series Editor: Jessica Cohn
Art Director: Sudakshina Basu
Designers: Joita Das and Prashant Kumar
Illustrators: Indranil Ganguly, Rishi Bhardwaj, Kusum Kala and Pooja Shukla
Photo research: Sejal Sehgal
Senior Project Manager: Ravneet Kaur
Project Manager: Shekhar Kapur

Printed in Malaysia
135642

Contents

Seeing the World

The world offers travelers plenty of contrasts in weather and culture. The different continents and their people also have many things in common. All around the world people eat some of the same kinds of food. Children go to school. People all over count the same way, though they do not use the same names for numbers. They all use math to make sense of the world.

Airport Math

Take a journey to see international math in action. It starts in North America, in the United States. At a New York City airport, the passengers of a London-bound plane check the numbers on their tickets and match them to the seats. Identifying numbers is one of the first kinds of math people learn. The passengers' luggage has been weighed. There must be a balance of fuel, passengers, and the items people bring aboard. Weights and measurement are math in action.

▼ The trip begins in New York City.

Airplane's Takeoff

At takeoff, the angle between the plane's nose and the ground increases.

* Diagram is not to scale.

The First Destination

The plane will cross the Atlantic Ocean to get to London, the capital of the United Kingdom. The United Kingdom, also known as Great Britain, is an island nation that is part of Europe. The pilots have onboard computers that do math for the flight. They track the plane's altitude, or height in the air. The pilots use math from takeoff to landing.

The flight attendant announces that the flight to London will take seven hours. Time is math, too. Math brings meaning to everything.

Calculation Station

A nonstop flight leaves John F. Kennedy International Airport, in New York, at 7 a.m. (Eastern Standard Time). It arrives at Heathrow International Airport in London seven hours later. London time (**Greenwich Mean Time**) is five hours ahead of the time in New York. What time will the plane arrive, in London time? (Answer is on page 31.)

Arriving in Europe

In London, the first stop is the famous London Bridge. The Romans built the original London Bridge about 2,000 years ago. The bridge was last rebuilt in 1973. To find out how long ago that was, take the current year and subtract 1973. For the year 2013, that would be 40 years.

European Measurements

The London Bridge allows cars and people to cross over the River Thames (pronounced: TEHMS). The bridge is 262 **meters** long. Meters are the basic unit of measurement used in Great Britain and many other countries. One meter equals about three feet plus three inches, which can be used to guess how long the bridge is in feet. A guess of 800 feet is pretty good. It is actually closer to 860 feet, but that is close enough for an estimate.

▲ London Bridge used to have houses on it. From 1758 to 1762, the bridge was cleared of buildings.

Hands-On Math: Build a Bridge

What You Will Need:

- Paper
- String or ribbon
- Tape
- Scissors
- 20 small items of similar weight, such as tiny toy cars, crayon halves, or keys

What to Do:

1 To begin, ask yourself:
- What are the different parts of a bridge that you will need to construct?
- Will you start with the roadway or with the arches?
- Will your bridge have cables?

2 You can build a bridge that is supported by braces underneath. Think about how you can roll and tape the paper.

3 You can build the roadway from the paper, ribbon, and tape.

4 You can also build a bridge that has towers and cables. You can build the cables from the ribbon and string.

Explain Away

What do you need to do to make a bridge that can support the weight of five items? What about twenty? (Answers are on page 31.)

Calculation Station

Suppose a young U.S. traveler has an allowance of $50 to spend in Paris. From one country to another, the units of money have different values. Units of money from one place are often worth more or less than those from other nations. So when traveling to other countries, it is wise to know the **exchange rate** you will get when you trade your money. Know how much of their money you will get in exchange for yours. In Paris, as throughout Europe, they use a unit of money called the **euro**. If one euro is equal to about $1.50, how many euros would the traveler have? (Answer is on page 31.)

▲ There are too many sidewalk cafes in Paris to count.

City of Lights

From London, the next stop is Paris, the capital of France. Paris is known as the "City of Lights." It was one of the first places to light its streets at night, and now it is ablaze with lights at night. After all, about a quarter of French workers live in the area. The term "City of Lights" has other meanings, too. It also refers to the city's beauty and the way the people celebrate thinking and the arts.

The Seine (SAYN) River divides the city into two separate regions. To the north of the river is the Rive Droite (REEV drawt), or the Right Bank. To the south of the river is the Rive Gauche (REEV gosh), or the Left Bank.

Rails Below Water

One way to get to Paris from London is on a train known as the Eurorail. How can that be if England is an island? The train goes under water in a huge tunnel that runs from the island of England to the main continent of Europe. The Channel Tunnel (called that because it is under the English Channel) is about 31 miles (50 kilometers) long.

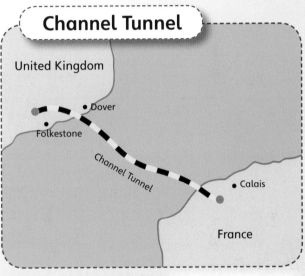

Channel Tunnel

United Kingdom

Dover

Folkestone

Channel Tunnel

Calais

France

* Diagram is not to scale.

The trip from London to Paris through the Channel Tunnel takes an hour and a half. If the train leaves London at 12:30 p.m., it gets to Paris at 2 p.m. However, Paris time is one hour ahead of London time. What time will the train arrive in Paris? When an hour gets added, it's 3 p.m.

◀ The Eurorail connects France and the United Kingdom.

Next Stop: Africa

After sightseeing in Europe, the journey leads to Africa. Africa is located partially in the **Northern Hemisphere** and partially in the **Southern Hemisphere**. The equator crosses right through a number of African countries—six, to be exact.

▶ The walls of the pyramids are four triangles.

Building with Math

In Africa, the first stop is the country of Egypt. More than 5,000 years ago, kings called pharaohs were in power in the region. They had huge pyramids built in their honor. Travelers still flock to see these structures today.

A pyramid is a **polyhedron** that has only one base. A polyhedron is a **three-dimensional** figure whose **faces** are **polygons**. Polygons are closed **two-dimensional** figures made of at least three lines.

The base of a pyramid is a square. The other faces of the structure are **congruent** triangles. They share a common **vertex**, which is the top point on a pyramid. The Egyptian pyramids each have a square base and four triangles as faces.

Calculation Station

To calculate the **volume** of a pyramid, first measure the sides and the height. Volume is the amount of space a three-dimensional object can hold. To measure that space in a pyramid, multiply the length of the base by the height of the structure. When you have the answer, multiply that by one-third.

What is the volume of a small model pyramid if its height is 5 inches and it has a square base that has sides of 8 inches? (Answer is on page 31.)

Ancient mathematicians used math to figure out how large the walls should be. Their figuring looked very different from ours. Unlike our Arabic number system, in which all numbers can be written using ten different **digits** (0, 1, 2, 3, 4, 5, 6, 7, 8, 9), ancient Egyptian math used only seven symbols in different combinations.

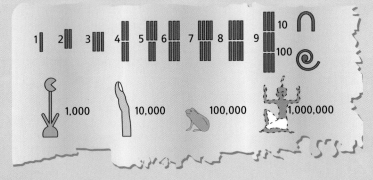

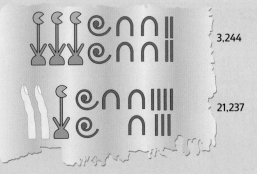

Can you read these numbers?

11

Kenyan Cows

The trip continues south, to Kenya. Here, they play a game that is like Mancala, which is found in the United States. Their game is called Giuthi (ghee-YOU-thee). Each game counter represents a cow.

Hands-On Math: Play Guithi

You can make a Guithi game board of your own.

What You Will Need:

- Empty egg carton
- 2 small bowls or cups
- 48 counters of the same kind (beans, pennies, buttons, shells)
- Partner

1 Side A belongs to Player One. Side B belongs to Player Two.

2 Set out a bowl for each player. These bowls are called sheds because they hold the counters, which stand for cows.

3 Place the counters evenly in the cups of the carton.

4 Player One first picks up all counters from one of the cups on his or her side. He or she moves either clockwise or counterclockwise to play.

5 Player One places one counter into each of the cups he or she passes. After placing the fourth counter, Player One picks up the counters in the cup in which the last counter was placed and starts all over again. This time, she or he moves in the opposite direction.

6 Player One continues until he or she places a counter into an empty cup. If the empty cup is on Player One's side, she or he continues playing. If the empty cup is on the opponent's side, it is Player Two's turn. Player Two chooses counters from one of the cups on his or her side and plays in a clockwise or counterclockwise direction, until a counter is placed in an empty cup on the opponent's side.

▼ Cows are a form of wealth in Kenya.

How to Capture Your Opponent's Counters:

Say one player has placed counters in the opponent's cups, and the last counter falls in an empty cup on the player's own side. Then the player is allowed to capture the counters in the cup directly opposite the empty cup. The player may continue to capture the opponent's counters. Capturing ends when the player comes to an occupied cup on the player's side of the board. It also ends if the opposite cup on the opponent's side is empty. Place the captured counters in the sheds.

To Win:

The game ends when no more counters are left to be moved. The player who has the most number of counters (or cattle) wins!

Explain Away

Is this game won by chance or thinking smart or both? (Answer is on page 31.)

Reaching Asia

The next stop on this global journey is the country of India, in the continent of Asia. The plane flies over the Himalayas to get there. The Himalayas are mountains in northern India. They are the home of the tallest mountain on Earth, called Mount Everest.

Mount Everest stands 29,028 feet (8,848 meters) high. Mountain climbers from all over the word travel here to try to reach its summit, or top.

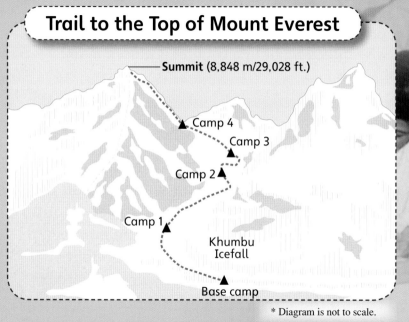

Trail to the Top of Mount Everest

Summit (8,848 m/29,028 ft.)

Camp 4

Camp 3

Camp 2

Camp 1

Khumbu Icefall

Base camp

* Diagram is not to scale.

A Capital City

From the snowy Himalayas, the plane continues to New Delhi, the capital of India. A traveler could spend all day counting people, cars, bicycles, motorcycles, and cows in New Delhi. With its big bright billboards and its mix of interesting old buildings and skyscrapers, the capital is filled with contrasts.

New Delhi is known for its great universities. In India, as in the United States, young students advance from nursery school to primary school to secondary school and beyond.

One story often repeated in the schools in India is a folktale that is also a math problem. Let's see if you can do the math.

▼ Vedic math was developed in India. Those are ancient shortcuts for solving math problems.

THERE ONCE LIVED A KING WHO HAD A BIG PROBLEM TO SOLVE. ONE BY ONE, PEOPLE FROM NEAR AND FAR HEARD THAT THE KING WAS IN NEED OF HELP, AND IN RETURN WOULD OFFER ANYTHING THEY DESIRED. HUNDREDS AND HUNDREDS OF IMPORTANT PEOPLE CAME TO TRY TO HELP THE KING, BUT IN THE END IT WAS A POOR, BUT VERY WISE MAN WHO SHOWED THE KING THE SOLUTION TO HIS PROBLEM.

"ASK FOR ANYTHING YOUR HEART DESIRES!" SAID THE KING TO THE MAN.

THE MAN THOUGHT FOR A WHILE AND SAID, "YOUR MAJESTY, I DO NOT NEED ALL THAT MUCH, BUT I WOULD LIKE ONE GRAIN OF RICE TODAY, TWO TOMORROW, FOUR THE NEXT DAY AND SO ON FOR A MONTH. EACH DAY, PLEASE DOUBLE THE NUMBER OF GRAINS YOU GAVE ME THE DAY BEFORE, AND I WILL BE MORE THAN SATISFIED."

THE KING WAS AGHAST. "THAT IS ALL YOU WANT? ABSOLUTELY! YOUR WISH IS MY COMMAND!"

Calculation Station

Figure out how many grains of rice the wise man got in 30 days. (Answer is on page 31.)

All the Way to China

From the bustling city of New Delhi, travel east to another major Asian destination, the country of China. More than a billion people live in China. It has more people than any other country. It is the fourth largest country in the world in terms of the **area** that it covers. China has 3.7 million square miles (9.6 million square kilometers).

Hitting the Wall

One of the most famous places in China is the Great Wall. This structure was built more than 2,000 years ago to protect China from invaders. Like the land around it, the shape of the Great Wall is not regular. It is wider at some spots than others. It is taller in places. The structure is said to be more than 2,000 miles (3,218 kilometers) long, but parts of it are in ruins.

▼ The Great Wall ranges from 15 to 50 feet (4.6 to 15 meters) high in different places.

Hands-On Math: Early Calculator

To make calculations in China, the **abacus** is still in use. The abacus is like a calculator without batteries. It can be used to add, subtract, multiply, and divide. The beads on the upper deck each have a value of five. The lower beads each have a value of 1. Move a bead to the center to count it.

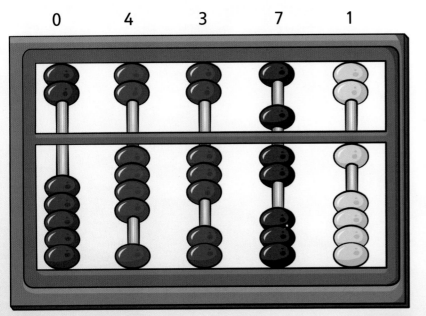

| 0 | 4 | 3 | 7 | 1 |

Each of these beads has a value of 5

Each of these beads has a value of 1

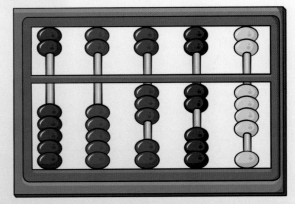

Ten millions	Millions	Hundred Thousands	Ten Thousands	Thousands	Hundred	Tens	Ones
0	0	0	0	4	3	7	1

Each column, from right to left, represents a different place value. What is place value? Think about the Arabic numbers we use. The ones are to the far right. Then come the tens. Next come the hundreds. This chart shows the Arabic number represented by the abacus at the top.

So, on the abacus next to the place value chart, the column to the far right represents the ones, the next one to the left represents the tens, then hundreds, and so on. Can you read the number? (Answer is on page 31.)

▲ China has the
world's largest
population.

Out on the Town

After visiting the Great Wall the next stop is the busy city of Beijing, the capital of China. Beijing has the largest public city square in the world, Tiananmen Square. The area of Tiananmen Square is 4.7 million square feet (440,000 square meters). It is said that this public space can hold a million people at one time. If you think about it, if each person had four square feet to stand in, there would still be nearly a million square feet left.

While waiting for food at a Beijing restaurant, you look at a Chinese magazine. You see a familiar puzzle.

Hands-On Math: Magic Squares

Magic squares are a favorite puzzle for people around the world.

What You Will Need:
- A few pieces of paper
- Pencil with eraser

What to Do:

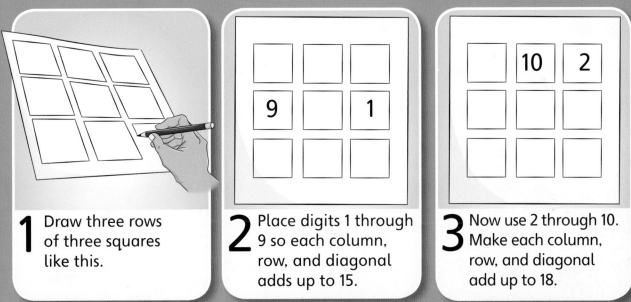

1 Draw three rows of three squares like this.

2 Place digits 1 through 9 so each column, row, and diagonal adds up to 15.

3 Now use 2 through 10. Make each column, row, and diagonal add up to 18.

Explain Away
What do you notice? What number is in the middle? How did you work through this challenge? (Answers are on page 31.)

The Land Down Under

The next stop is the "land down under." Australia is a continent that is completely in the Southern Hemisphere. It is located south from, or "down under," the equator.

Make It Melbourne

The journey leads to the city of Melbourne. This building is one of the extraordinary examples of tiling in Melbourne. To do tiling, artists fill a flat space, such as a wall, with tiles. A variety of tile shapes can be used. The tiles can be rectangular, triangular, or an **irregular polygon**. Someone who is good at tiling is good at math.

▼ Federation Square, in Melbourne, has great examples of tiling.

Hands-On Math: Make Your Own Tiling

Using shapes the way you do in tiling is called **tessellation**. It can be done with any polygon, as long as there are no gaps or overlaps.

What You Will Need:
- Small square piece of paper
- Large rectangular sheet of paper
- Eraser
- Colored pencils or crayons
- Pencil

What to Do:

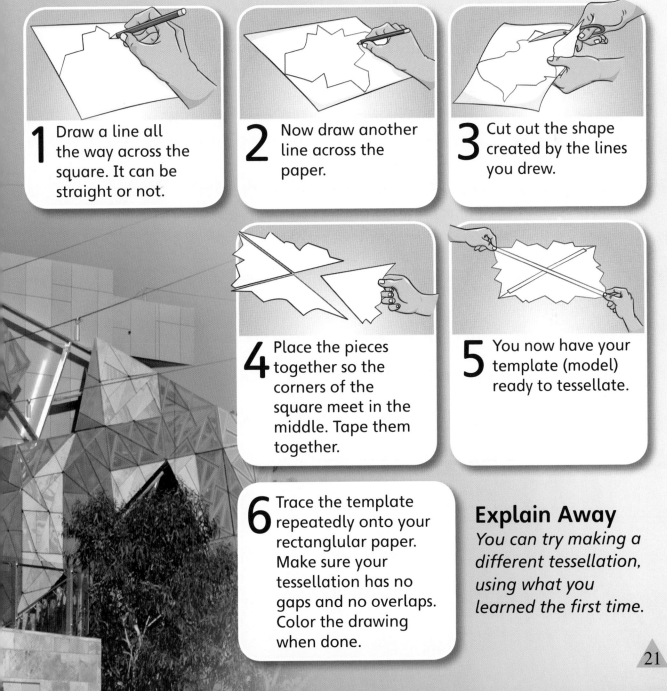

1 Draw a line all the way across the square. It can be straight or not.

2 Now draw another line across the paper.

3 Cut out the shape created by the lines you drew.

4 Place the pieces together so the corners of the square meet in the middle. Tape them together.

5 You now have your template (model) ready to tessellate.

6 Trace the template repeatedly onto your rectanglular paper. Make sure your tessellation has no gaps and no overlaps. Color the drawing when done.

Explain Away
You can try making a different tessellation, using what you learned the first time.

21

Swinging to South America

After Australia comes the continent of South America. The plane flies directly to the country of Peru. The journey continues by car to the city of Cuzco. That is the old capital city of the ancient Incan empire. From there a train takes passengers to see the ancient civilization of Machu Picchu, also known as the "Lost City."

Getting There

On the train, the travelers study a map, deciding when to get off. The train can leave them at an old trail to the hidden city. Or it can take them closer to the ruins. The trail is part of an old road system. The Inca had a system of roads that reached from Ecuador in the north to Chile in the south.

The roads include paths to Machu Picchu. The key on the map gives an idea of the distance they would have to walk. This key is in **kilometers**. A kilometer (km) is a unit of distance used in the metric system of measurement. One kilometer is equal to about one-half mile.

Many visitors take a four-day hike, from Km 88 to the ruins. The first day usually leads to Wayllabamba. Using the key, that seems to be about 10 kilometers (6 miles).

Trail to Machu Picchu

PUENTE RUINAS

AGUASCALIENTES

0 1 2Km

Torontoy

Rio Urubamba

Km 88

Chachabamba

Liactapata

Rio Pacamayo

Choquesuysuy

Rio Kusichaca

Phuyupatamarica

Tambo de Runkuracay

Sayaqmarka

WAYLLABAMBA

* Diagram is not to scale.

Calculation Station

The tour of the ruins includes a tour guide's stories about the Inca and Peru. One story is a math riddle that he tells for fun: A man was returning from the market in Peru with a fox, a guinea pig, and a bag of chicken feed. On the way home he had to cross a river. There was an old bridge across the river. To cross the bridge, he had to hold the handrail with one hand and carry one of his belongings with the other hand. This way he could carry only one item at a time. If he carried the fox across the bridge first, the guinea pig would eat the chicken feed. If he carried the chicken feed across first, the fox would eat the guinea pig. How did he manage to carry everything across the bridge? (Answer is on page 31.)

▼ Machu Picchu was built 22,966 feet (7,000 meters) above sea level.

23

The Last Stop Is Antarctica

This continent provides plenty of contrast to the others. Antarctica is the coldest and windiest continent on Earth. Some kinds of penguins live here, as do different types of seals. There are no trees or bushes to be seen, but there is a mix of fungus and algae called lichen. The main thing on this continent is ice! The Antarctic ice cap has nearly 7 million **cubic miles** (29 million **cubic kilometers**) of ice. This is 90 percent of all the ice on Earth.

Water World

The ice on Antarctica holds between 60 percent and 70 percent of all of the world's fresh water. The odd thing is that Antarctica is still considered a desert. In scientific terms, a desert is a region that has less than ten inches of rainfall per year. This continent has that little rain.

Most deserts are hot. As a result, they have high levels of **evaporation**. That is when a solid or a liquid, like seawater, becomes vapor. There is very little evaporation from the continent of Antarctica. So old snow and ice pile up.

Calculation Station

Make a line graph charting the monthly temperature at McMurdo Station in Antarctica. Put the months of the year on the horizontal axis (line going across). Along the vertical axis (line going up and down), label the temperature. Use the information provided here. (Answer is on page 31.)

	McMurdo Station, Antarctica
January	0
February	-6
March	-14
April	-17
May	-19
June	-19
July	-21
August	-22
September	-20
October	-15
November	-6
December	0

▲ Scientists keep track of the penguin population.

Seeing a New Way

On the plane headed back to New York, a channel on the in-flight video screen shows a map. The route of the plane is shown with a red line on the map. The red line grows longer the entire time the plane is flying. When the plane lands, the line will finally be defined. It will have two end points, the start and the finish.

Looking out the window, the geography of the planet is on full display. When people think about mountains, they usually picture these landforms from the side. They think about how high the mountains are. From the plane, the perspective of the passengers changes. They look down over mountains, oceans, farmland, and clouds. They think about the world as a whole.

◀ The curvature of the Earth can be seen at high altitudes.

Hands-On Math: Your World

Here is a fun way to make your own globe, little by little, over a week or so.

What You Will Need:
- Round balloon (inflated)
- Lots of newspaper
- 1 cup flour
- Water
- Old plastic container for mixing glue
- Spoon or stick to stir the glue

- Pencil
- Blue and green tempera paint
- Paint brushes
- Black marker
- Globe or world map

What to Do:

1 With an adult, mix 1 cup of flour into 1 cup of water until the mixture is thin and runny. Stir into 4 cups of hot water. Let it cool.

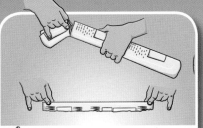

2 Tear newspaper into 1-inch wide strips. Dip each strip in the flour glue, and wrap the strip around the balloon.

3 Place one layer of strips around the entire balloon. Let that layer dry overnight. Make at least three layers over three nights.

4 Draw a dot for each of the poles. Next draw the continent you live in. Then draw the other continents.

5 Paint the continents green. Let that dry. Use blue paint for bodies of water. Let that dry.

6 Outline the equator and continents with dark marker. You can write the ocean names, too.

Note: Work carefully, so as not to burst the balloon.

Back Home

The trip ends where it began, at a New York City airport. Yet the calculations continue! Some travelers will be driven home in a limousine or a taxi. They check to see if they have money to tip the driver. If the cost will be $50, and they want to tip 10 percent, they will need $55.

▲ U.S. airlines carry more than 500 million passengers yearly.

InVision

In the airport, there is often a bank where people can exchange their money from other lands. A sign at the teller's window lists the exchange rates among forms of money, such as the euro, peso, or U.S. dollar. On another airport wall hang six clocks, each displaying the time from a different city in the world: New York, London, Paris, Sydney, Tokyo, and Bombay. Some travelers are entering a time zone later or earlier than the one they just left. Math will help them figure out how much sleep they will get that night. Math is a tool you can take with you everywhere, to help get the most out of life.

Calculation Station

If your suitcase weighed 20 pounds at the start, but you collected souvenirs of the following weights from each continent, how much would the suitcase weigh at the end?

Europe: 3 pounds

Egypt: 5 pounds

Kenya: 4 pounds

Asia: 6 pounds

Australia: 3 pounds

South America: 7 pounds

Antarctica: 0 pounds, nothing purchased!

(Answer is on page 31.)

Glossary

abacus Ancient calculator made of shifting beads in rows.

area Measure of the surface of a two-dimensional or three-dimensional figure.

congruent Having exactly the same size and shape.

cubic kilometer Kilometer with three dimensions (length, width, and height) measured in the metric unit of distance the kilometer.

cubic mile Mile in three dimensions (length, width, and height) measured in the unit of distance the mile.

digit One of the number symbols (0, 1, 2, 3, 4, 5, 6, 7, 8 ,9).

euro Unit of money used throughout most of Europe.

evaporation Process where a liquid changes to gas or vapor (like when water boils and turns into steam).

exchange rate The difference in value of two types of money.

face One side of a solid or three-dimensional figure; the plane figure of that side.

Greenwich Mean Time The time in London, England.

irregular polygon Polygon with sides that are not the same length.

kilometer Unit of the metric system that measures distance.

meter Unit of the metric system that measures length.

Northern Hemisphere Part of Earth that is north of the equator.

polygon Two-dimensional closed figure made of at least three lines.

polyhedron Three-dimensional figure whose faces are polygons.

sea level At ocean surface when water is between low and high tide.

Southern Hemisphere Part of the Earth that is south of the equator.

tessellation Arrangement of shapes in a plane without overlaps or gaps.

three-dimensional Having three dimensions: length, width, and height.

two-dimensional Having two dimensions: width and height.

vertex Point at which two line segments, lines, or rays meet.

volume Amount of space a three-dimensional figure can hold.

Answer Key

Calculation Station

p. 5: The plane arrives in London at 7 p.m. (Greenwich Mean Time).

p. 8: Since 1 euro = $1.50, and you have $50, divide 50 by 1.50, or 33.34 euros.

p. 11: The volume of the pyramid is approximately 13.3 (8 × 5 = 40 and 40 ÷ 3 = 13.33) square inches.

p. 15: Day 1: 1

Day 2: 1 + 1 = 2

Day 3: 2 × 2 = 2 × 2 = 4

Day 4: 4 × 4 = 16

Day 5 = 16 × 16 = 256

On the thirtieth day, the man will receive 1,073,741,824 rice grains. That's about 1 billion grains of rice!

p. 23: He carried the guinea pig across first, because he knew the fox wouldn't eat the chicken feed. He then carried the chicken feed over the bridge and brought back the guinea pig, because he didn't want the guinea pig to eat the chicken feed. He then carried the fox over as he knew the fox wouldn't eat the chicken feed. He then went back to get the guinea pig.

p. 25:

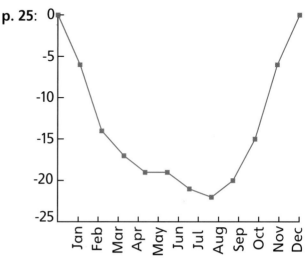

p. 29: 28 lbs. of souvenirs + 20 lbs. (original weight) = 48 lbs.

Hands-On Math

p. 7: You might find out that braces are better when bigger. You might realize that you can hang a walkway and that it is especially sturdy the more "cables" are used to hold it up. Many solutions exist.

pp. 12-13: Some luck helps, but thinking helps more. One good strategy is hoarding the pieces. Another is moving quickly to try to confuse your partner.

p. 17: 324.

p. 19: Here is one possible answer to the magic square challenge where each row, column, and diagonal adds up to 15.

4	3	8
9	5	1
2	7	6

Here is a possibility for digits 2 through 10, adding to 18:

6	10	2
4	5	9
8	3	7

31

Index